Anna Theresa Wendel

Narration in Robert Louis Stevenson's "The Strange Case of Dr. Jekyll and Mr. Hyde"

GRIN Verlag

Bibliografische Information der Deutschen Nationalbibliothek:

Die Deutsche Bibliothek verzeichnet diese Publikation in der Deutschen National-
bibliografie; detaillierte bibliografische Daten sind im Internet über http://dnb.d-
nb.de/ abrufbar.

Imprint:

Copyright © 2012 GRIN Verlag GmbH
Druck und Bindung: Books on Demand GmbH, Norderstedt Germany
ISBN: 978-3-656-35984-5

This book at GRIN:

http://www.grin.com/en/e-book/208470/narration-in-robert-louis-stevenson-s-the-
strange-case-of-dr-jekyll-and

GRIN - Your knowledge has value

Der GRIN Verlag publiziert seit 1998 wissenschaftliche Arbeiten von Studenten, Hochschullehrern und anderen Akademikern als eBook und gedrucktes Buch. Die Verlagswebsite www.grin.com ist die ideale Plattform zur Veröffentlichung von Hausarbeiten, Abschlussarbeiten, wissenschaftlichen Aufsätzen, Dissertationen und Fachbüchern.

Visit us on the internet:

http://www.grin.com/

http://www.facebook.com/grincom

http://www.twitter.com/grin_com

WS 2009/10

FB II - Anglistik

30.01.2012

Narration
in Robert Louis Stevenson's
The Strange Case of Dr. Jekyll and Mr. Hyde

Anna Theresa Wendel

Bachelor of Education

Table of Content

1. Introduction

This term paper deals with the analysis of the narration in the novel "The Strange Case of Dr. Jekyll and Mr. Hyde" written by Robert Louise Stevenson in 1886. First, I will analyze the narrative situation by elaborating on the narrative structure of the story and its effect on the reader. Then I want to examine the reliability of the different narrators in the book. In the end I will summarize my results by drawing a short conclusion.

2. Narrative Situation

In the following, I will explain the multiperspectival narrative situation in the novel by pointing out the different perspectives, namely those of Enfield, Utterson, Lanyon and Jekyll. Afterwards, I will analyze the effect and the purpose that this narrative construction has on the reader.

2.1 Narrative Structure

The beginning of the novel is told by an authorial narrator who "offers a godlike panoramic view from an Olympic position outside and above the story" (Meyer 66). Also the characters are introduced by this omniscient voice, for example Mr. Utterson who is described in a very detailed way. Furthermore, on the first page, the thoughts of people (here Mr. Utterson's and Mr.Enfield's) are presented which is also a hint for an omniscient perspective. During one of their "Sunday walks" (1), Mr. Enfield tells "a very odd story" (1) to his friend Utterson in first-person narration. Because Utterson is the one who is addressed we already see the story from his point of view. The fact that he, and also the reader, is not satisfied by Enfield's explanation sets the story going (Niederhoff 32). From chapter 2 onwards, the story is told by an undefined narrator but the reader goes along with

Utterson's perspective. He functions as a reflector, due to this, we see the scenes through his eyes (Meyer 67).

In chapter 4 *The Carew Murder Case*, a maid tells that a "crime of singular ferocity" (14) happened in London. The account is also told in the figural narrative situation by an invisible narrator but the event is presented through Utterson's point of view. The question arises how the lawyer is connected to the maid's experiences. But it can be suggested that she must have told the story several times, not only to the police: "she used to say, with streaming tears, when she narrated that experience" (14). Probably this is how Utterson heard about the incident. Another answer is that he was called by the police because he was somehow involved (15).

Besides Mr.Enfield's *Story of the Door* and the maid's report of the Carew Murder, two other narrations are inserted into the main one, namely *Dr. Lanyon's Narrative* and *Henry Jekyll's Full Statement of the Case*. In addition, many documents, such as Jekyll's will, play an important role for the narrative structure of the novel: "the novel is composed (...) of ten disparate documents identified only as letters, incidents, cases and statements" (Thomas 160). Garrett also points out: "What is most striking about them is, rather, the ways they are all shaped to fit together like the pieces of a puzzle (...)" (60).

In chapter 6, the letter in which Dr. Hastie Lanyon confides to Utterson what he had found out about Jekyll is introduced. Since Utterson is not allowed to open it until the death of Jekyll, we have no insight until chapter 9 which is called *Dr. Lanyon's Narrative*, and consists of the letter. Therefore, Lanyon is the first-person narrator who explains his own death and "reveals the identity of Jekyll and Hyde, leaving to Jekyll's the task of explanation." (Garrett 60).

The last chapter, *Henry Jekyll's Full Statement of the Case*, also starts immediately with the letter Jekyll left for his lawyer Utterson and thus is in the first-person narrative situation. He is the experiencing-I, but during his narrative, he switches several times from first to third person. Firstly, he talks in the first person about himself, regardless of whether he is Jekyll or Hyde, but then he suddenly starts to mention Hyde and sometimes himself in third person: "(...) where Jekyll perhaps might have succumbed, Hyde rose to the importance of that moment." (51). A few lines later, he explains, "He, I say – I cannot say, I."(52). Only when he turns into Henry Jekyll again, he speaks in the first person once more. In the last sentence he even speaks of himself as Henry Jekyll in the third person: "as I lay down the pen, (...), I bring the life of that unhappy Henry Jekyll to an end."(54). Also Garrett stresses this feature: "As narrator and author of his "Statement", Jekyll is "I", but as protagonist or object of his narrative he is sometimes "I", sometimes "he" or "Jekyll", while "Hyde" is sometimes replaced by "I"" (Garrett 62). The scientist distances himself from both of his identities, he "cannot take authority for his own actions or even for his own words" (Thomas 75). The more power Hyde takes over him, the more he distances himself verbally. According to Thomas, the "end of *Jekyll and Hyde* is the fragmenting of the self into distinct pieces with distinct voices, not the bringing together of those pieces into some unified character who speaks with a single voice." (73) and Saposnik calls the last chapter the "culmination of the multiple- narrative technique" (724). Finally, Jekyll's letter ends with his own death: "(...) the voice of Jekyll is silenced, replaced by the texts he has written." (Thomas 73) and it is also "the last document Utterson and the reader view" (Clunas 178), so we do not learn the full story until the lawyer does.

What this all amounts to, is that, all characters contribute to discover some parts of the story, but on the whole, the novel is about what Utterson inquires about the case. This also applies to the last two chapters which only consist of the letters from Lanyon and Jekyll and which are just unveiled to him and the reader when he withdraws to his office to read them (Niederhoff 40): „Utterson, once more leaving the servants gathered about the fire in the hall, trudged back to his office to read the two narratives in which this mystery was now to be explained." (35).

Moreover, the events are not told in chronological order and the story is supplemented by three first-person narrations which are all embedded into the overall structure of the main narrative which is a third-person narration focusing on Mr.Utterson's point of view. "These first person narratives are not textually "framed" by that of the third person because the latter does not continue. However, they are chronologically framed by the main sequence." (Clunas 178).

2.2 Effect on the Reader

The plot starts with Mr. Enfield's narrative which sets the story going and provides the main reason for Mr. Utterson to do research on Hyde's identity. This story is told in direct speech what makes the story alive and catches the reader's attention right at the beginning. Then, the reader goes along with the lawyer's point of view and he can only assume that further reading will reveal more: Utterson is "the vehicle of the reader's curiosity" (Clunas 177) and we as readers get the impression that we "share the thoughts, feelings and perceptions of a character." (Meyer 67). Stevenson chose the perspective of a person who is not involved in the secret of Dr. Jekyll, therefore, suspense can be created. Moreover, because of the fact that he does not believe in irrationalism, it does not come to his mind that something supernatural happened to his friend Jekyll. In nearly the whole novel, he, and with him the reader, is not aware of the truth, so this gives both the possibility to make their own speculations. Not until the last two chapters, when he reads the letters of Lanyon and Jekyll, they come to know the denouement of the case. In addition, this letters and also the other narratives have another function: "The total text, then, is constituted by an array of overlapping narratives that move us back and forth in time, permitting us to re-read certain key scenes from a new perspective." (Clunas 178).

Besides Mr.Utterson's point of view, we experience three other perspectives which deliver additional information and give a more personal dimension to the story. At first, the maid's account of the murder: her description is very emotional and in addition, she faints when narrating it (vgl. p.15). This has the same effect as Dr. Lanyon's letter: both narrations stress the cruelty of the crime and transmit a feeling of horror. The doctor's narrative is very dramatic, because what he describes, namely Dr. Jekyll's transformation inot Hyde, provoked his death. Furthermore, even after giving his version of the story, the reader remain in the dark as to how and why this situation came about, because he does not write down the reasons.

Finally, in the last chapter, everything falls into place when Dr. Jekyll provides his confession. Through adding his version, the reader can understand all connections, especially between the documents. He also becomes aware of the scientist's inner motives for his action and has the possibility to reflect the story on another basis of knowledge what may change his position and lead him to "revise his understanding of what is going on at any given point of the narrative" (Clunas 178). Furthermore, this way of narration draws out the suspense and through this chosen structure, a very dramatic ending could be created: "Nothing in the story is as singly frightening as Henry Jekyll's final narrative, for it is there that the reader learns most about the distorted mind which released an unwilling Hyde." (Saposnik 722).

3. Reliability

In this section, I want to discuss the narrative's reliability throughout the novel. "In contrast to other multiple narratives whose several perspectives often raise questions of subjective truth and moral ambiguity, these individual narratives in *The Strange Case of Dr. Jekyll and Mr. Hyde* provide a linear regularity of information." (Saposnik 722). According to this statement, the different narratives in the story can be considered as reliable what is also supported by the fact that the events are coherent and without any logical gaps.

Additionally, the main narrator is a detached heterodiegetic one (Niederhoff 40) what means that he generally "inspires confidence" (Meyer 70) and we do not have serious reasons to distrust him. Furthermore he is portrayed as a noble and respectable man who uses a factual and dry tone what ensures objectivity. In contrast to that, the maid's account seems to be kind of subjective, because she is depicted as a naïve and emotional person. Nevertheless, her description of Hyde goes along with those of the others, so she must be reliable in some way.

Although the events are not told in chronological order, they are coherent because one event leads to another. Moreover, certain events or characters are described from different points of view what increases the reliability of the narration. For example the appearance of Mr. Hyde is characterized several times throughout the novel and everybody saw him with some kind of deformation but cannot explain it (4/10).

The other narratives, namely those of Enfield, Lanyon and Jekyll, are all first person narration what could be a reason to distrust their reliability. Since there are no contradictions in their narratives, the different versions match with each other. Beyond that, we have a change from third person to first person narrative and that offers the reader some guarantee of truth because the first-person narrative only confirms what has already been told earlier. Therefore, the whole story is consistent what proves reliability. Besides, the different documents serve as pieces of evidence.

Only Jekyll as narrator could not be reliable at all, because he as the Experiencing-I, is directly involved in his narrative and we must also call his mental ability into question, because he himself mentions that he has "lost his identity" (54). However, he calls his statement a confession whatsuggest reliability at least at some stage.

4. Conclusion

In summary it can be said, that Stevenson's novel *The Strange Case of Dr.Jekyll and Mr. Hyde* shows a complex narrative structure, not only through the sequence of actions but also through the different narrators and documents which are interwoven with the whole story. As I have tried to show above, it is difficult to say whether the characters are reliable or not, but certainly is that the narrative is consistent and coherent.

5. Bibliographie

Primary Source

- Stevenson, Robert Louis. *The Strange Case of Dr. Jekyll and Mr.Hyde*. New York: Dover Publications, 1991. Print.

Secondary Sources

Books/Journal Articles:

- Clunas, Alex. "Comely External Utterance: Reading Space in The Strange Case of Dr. Jekyll and Mr. Hyde." *Journal of Narrative Technique* 24.3 (1994):173-89. Print.
- Dölvers, Horst. *Der Erzähler Robert Louis Stevenson*. Bern: Francke Verlag, 1969. Print.
- Garrett, Peter K.. "Cries and Voices: Reading Jekyll and Hyde" *D[octo]r Jekyll and M[iste]r Hyde after one hundred years*(1988): 59-72.Print.
- Meyer, Michael. *English and American Literatures.*3. Auflage. Tübingen: A. Francke Verlag, 2008. Print.
- Niederhoff, Burkhard. *Erzähler und Perspektive bei Robert Louis Stevenson.* Würzburg: Königshausen und Neumann, 1994. Print.
- Saposnik, Irving S. "The Anatomy of "Dr. Jekyll and Mr. Hyde"" *Studies in English Literature* 11.4 (1971):715-31. Print.
- Thomas, Ronald R.. "In the Company of Strangers: Absent Voices in Stevenson's "Dr. Jekyll and Mr. Hyde" Beckett's "Company"" *Modern Fiction Studies* 32.2 (1986): 157-173. Print.
- Thomas, Ronald R.. "The Strange Voices in the Strange Case: Dr.Jekyll, Mr.Hyde, and the Voices of Modern Fiction" *D[octo]r Jekyll and M[iste]r Hyde after one hundred years* (1988): 73-93. Print.